pictureshowpress.net

Cover Image Credit: David Cieslikowski
Author Image Credit: Sharon De La O

FIRST EDITION

ISBN-13: 978-1-7341702-9-0

ALONG THE FAULT LINE

TAMARA MADISON

Picture Show Press

To the memory of my father, who developed the farm that nurtured me, and my mother, who endured it.

"All the animals on the ground want to kill you, and all the plants carry knives."

– Douglas Benezra

"I have always loved the desert. One sits down on a desert sand dune, sees nothing, hears nothing. Yet through the silence something throbs, and gleams..."

– Antoine de Saint-Exupéry, The Little Prince

POEMS

Walters

It used to be called Walters,
this little stagecoach stop
just west of the fault line.
Someone in a mood of whimsy
gave the station Moorish arches.
A world traveler stopped by
on his way to the coast
and remembered his visit
to another desert far away.
He thought the place
could use a better name
and that's how this dusty
nub of a town in the middle
of a sweltering desert,
parched and plagued by gnats,
came to be called Mecca.

The Pink House

There's a line like a bathtub ring
at the mountain's base, above
the alluvial fan; there are seashells too.
purple-tinged, brittle, long embedded
in sand. Once this was a sea.

Fan palms line the fault where upheaval
scattered rocks, formed hills and canyons
and stained them pink, brown and rust.
My family lived here once.

And where our pink house stood with its store
of artifacts – my name writ backwards
on the bottom of a drawer,
the left-handed kitchen my mother designed,
the swirling lights of my father's ghost
– a slab of concrete remains,

time-scarred, sulfate-red,
rusted ruddy with the blood of memory.

Xerophile

(with thanks to W.B. Yeats)

I come from a dry place.
I live in a dry place.
I am a dry place.
I hold my water tight.

My leaves grow hairs
to trap the ghost
of water that appears
after sundown
when xerophiles
reveal themselves
in scent.

I keep my scent inside.
None will ever know
my water.
I hold all of it
here
in my deep heart's core.

Sand Verbena

Mine is a pale land:
pale sky, pale sand,
pale sun-bleached everything.
My playground was bare sand
studded with stone and shell
from a long-dead sea.
Playmates were lizards
and quail, playthings rocks
and my own thoughts.
Some years, winter watered
seeds that slept in the sand,
then spring covered the dunes
with purple verbena, low-growing
flowers with furry leaves
and furry stems. I made bouquets,
stumbled over dry gullies
to give them to Mother – a clutch
of sweet-smelling blossoms
that sagged in my sweaty hands.

En Memoria

It was sand when my father bought the land across a canal from a clump of colorful hills along the fault line. With an artful mix of chemicals, he coaxed the sandy soil to yield 80 acres of citrus trees that bloomed sweetly in spring and trimmed themselves by Christmas with baubles of orange and yellow. Across the gravel road the desert, raw and veined by winter rain, sprouted spindly smoke trees, creosote, purple verbena. In time, other farms – grapes, tomatoes, vegetables – appeared in the sand surrounding ours, and beyond those farms sometimes dumping grounds appeared. Old mattresses sprouted rusted wire coils. Bald tires rotted in the sun. Baby strollers missing wheels filled with dirt. Doorless ovens gaped. Leather boots folded in the summer heat. A dog's paw reached up from the sand. Rattlesnakes left tracks as they wound among the corpses of household objects.

Once I came upon an oval of stones headed by a cross made from fence pickets. *En Memoria* read the faded hand-drawn sign; time had erased anything written below. The oval seemed small, maybe five feet long, not much more. A farm worker, surely; no doubt from Mexico. I imagined a little man, sun-brown, with an Aztec nose. How did he die? Flu? Snake bite? A disease no one knew he had until it was too late? A farm accident? Murder? I wondered if anyone had notified his next of kin, and I thought of him there, wrapped in nothing but a blanket and laid in the dirt like a dead dog. I thought of him every time I went near there, a nameless arrangement of bones in a cemetery of discarded effects. At night the stars were so bright you could almost hear them crackle. By day the sun punched the desert like a thug, rotting mattresses, ovens, tractor tires, work boots; this nameless immigrant lay there among them while buzzards circled overhead, unaware that he had ever lived or died.

Mud Pies

The sand drinks water from the hose;
I can even hear it gulping. It is wet
and grainy as I smooth it into tins.
Our pink house is at my back, the sandy
lake of our driveway studded with rocks.
She drives up in a white car. She wears
a yellow dress and a big smile beneath
the white hat. I know her; she is my first
friend. I have spent two years on this earth,
yet still I never talk. Even my family
has yet to hear my first word. But I know
this person. She will accept the invitation,
so I ask: *Mrs. Thomas, would you like
to make mud pies with me?* Her mouth opens
wide with surprise and a smile. *Why sure!*
she says, and settles onto the sand beside me.
We smooth the pies with wet sandy hands,
I in bare feet, she in her yellow dress.
It is her idea to place a yellow flower
in the center of each pie. She'll go in to see
my mother when she's ready. For now,
there are three more tins to fill,
and a handful of flowers to place on top.

Bougainvillea

She is brown like her shadow
on hot ground at high noon.
Her hair, a dark bush, bounces
atop her busy torso as she steps –
snap snap – in rubber thongs
in the pummeling sun
of a desert afternoon. Her arms
are sinewy-thin, muscular
("from beating children"
she says). When I sob
as Mommy leaves for wood shop
or a meeting, she snaps to the crib
and shakes me, the wailing child:
If you don't stop that right now
I'll beat you to a bloody pulp!
Her sunglasses flare out
toward her temples like the sly
outspoken fins on the powder-blue
Mercury that she steers
with the same hand that holds
the Reader's Digest while the other
applies Bougainvillea Red
lipstick; a billowing fan of dust
rises behind the speeding car
where we children sit
on the sticky vinyl back seat,
secure in our mother's love.
Sometimes at night she fastens
rhinestones to her ears and poufs on
pungent green perfume, sets
the cummerbund on Dad's tuxedo;
he looks like a movie star
with all the crop dust washed away.
We watch them drive off

toward a lurid sunset
of blazing orange and pink
and night grows around the purple
shoulders of the mountains,
smelling of dirt and work
and farm chemicals.

Cocktail Party, circa 1960

At the party my mother sits at the bar
by the dial phone, smiling for the camera.
In the foreground there are martini glasses
and open bottles of liquor, but my mother
looks sober, smooth-faced and young,
one chiffon strap sliding down
her suntanned shoulder. She's wearing
her original nose and large clustered
rhinestone earrings. In the darkened
background my father sits watching her
as though she's a fantastic, wild creature
he's afraid might get away. But why
would the hen leave the handsomest
fox in the room? He's honest, a good
provider. She has seen his soft parts.
He hopes she will forgive him.

Child Writer

Beyond the dark window
quake-wrinkled hills
recline under moonlight

A few stars wink
An owl hoots
Coyotes on the dunes
sing a scratchy song

From the living room
the Bonanza theme
taps at my ear

I sit cozy at my desk
with paper, pen,
and an idea.

Ace

The postmaster drove a Cadillac
with the design of an ace
on each taillight. He was a big door
of a man, with matching wife.
We sat with Ace, my mother and I,
on the steps of the pool.
Ace took me on his lap
and as they chatted, his fingers
moved beneath my ballerina
swimsuit, until they found
that special spot between my legs.
I couldn't swim yet, but quietly
freed myself and floated away
in my bright orange float coat.
After that when we picked up
the mail I hid behind my mother.
She continued to joke with Ace
and his wife, comfortable and friendly,
the way one does in a small town
where everyone thinks they know
everyone's business.

¡Colese, Colá!

Patty taught me how to lie,
how to hide from the teacher
and knock
using rocks
on the kindergarten door.

Patty taught me how to say
"You ain't the boss of me!"
how to pull a hair
from my arm
so we could become
blood sisters.
Patty showed me the place
where her dad
kicked in the door.

We colored in books
'til our knuckles
turned purple-green.
We shared our lunch
on the seesaw.
We decided to speak Spanish
because everybody else did
and she made up the words
I'll never forget:
¡Colese, Colá!

I missed her
when she moved
back to Alaska
but there she was again
in the seventh grade –
friendly, plump
and warm as sunshine
with a garland of hickeys
circling her neck.

The Salton Sea

We used to water ski there,
my mother and brother cruising
over the wake, he leaning
shoulder to the salt-thick sea;
my sister and I gripping the rope,
bouncing along in the wake,
pretending it was fun; our father,
a monolith rising, scowling,
from the water, the edifice
of his body crashing back
into the brine. In time, the water
grew brown and gave off
a fetid smell. Corvina began
to arrive, long, white, belly-up
dry-gilled, along the muddy
shore and we soon found water
elsewhere. But from our living
room, if I stood tall, I could still
see that foul cesspool of a lake
shimmering in the sunlight.

Her Name Was Becky

The morning after our dog barked, barked,
barked into the darkness, a row of cars
appears on the side of the road at the half mile
turn. The cars are there all day, windows
glinting in the sunlight, and men in dress
trousers with big cameras prowl around
in the dirt on the edge of the neighbor's farm.
My parents do not say why, if they even know.
The next day, Mother hands me an article:
A girl from another town, Becky Sayers
is her name, a girl about my age, ten,
found dead in a ditch. Something about a man
and a car outside of a store in Brawley,
something about puppies. Then, "Officers
have not determined whether it was a sexual
assault." I don't know what that means,
but perhaps something in those words
can tell me why Mother has given it
to me to read instead of telling me herself.
I hold the yellow square like a puzzle
my eyes can hardly fathom.

Sears Catalog

We'd call each other when it came.
From the kitchen telephones in our homes
five dusty, farm-chemical-soaked miles apart
we'd divvy up the pages: everything on the left
mine, everything on the right, Lori's.
We'd skip the power tools and appliances
and go for the housewares, clothes and toys.
If I liked the dad in the forest green wool coat
with the fleece lining, she'd trade him
for the dad in the navy Scandinavian sweater.
She'd choose the Batman costume worn
by the little blond boy and I'd trade it
for the princess gown with the silver tiara
that she said looked silly. When we disagreed,
we sometimes might make an exchange,
like the plaid skirt for the two long-sleeved blouses,
one checkered with a cowgirl yoke, the other striped.
We got our moms new sheets and curtains,
and from the children's section we'd sometimes trade
the kids for new siblings and ignore the clothes.
We'd trade boys' toys, girls' toys, guns and ammo,
shower curtains, and even, if we were in the mood,
couches and toilets. After an hour or so of trading,
someone would need the phone and realize
how long we'd been on it. We'd hand over
the receiver, sticky and hot from use,
and plan to finish the next day where we'd left off.
This went on until the time she made me mad.
I got back at her by telling someone else
about the secret language we'd made up.
When we came around to being friends again,
something happened that my parents
didn't tell me about and we moved away,
leaving behind a friendship sealed
between the pages of a Sears catalog.

Treehouse

My father nailed some plywood
up in the mulberry tree
so I could have a treehouse.

I spent many lonely summer days
among the dusty mulberry leaves
reading and watching ants crawl
along the branches. If I climbed higher

I could see the train snake along
the valley floor, watch vultures
circling in the pale desert sky.

In time, I saw that the tree's flesh
had begun to grow around the nails
and the plywood too; the tree accepted
this addition as part of its life story.

Saving the Lemons

When the air drops low
on a winter night and we know
the mountains are expecting
snow, my dad and brother rise
in the dark to flood the fields
and save the crop from frost.
In the morning the water
between the rows of trees
has grown a skin of ice,
not strong enough to bear
our weight, nor room enough
to walk or skate, but
we can touch our toes
to its brittle face and marvel
at what water can become.
When the yellow bus
comes up the gravel road
we run with icy breath; school
awaits us all, even my brother
who was up late in the night
to save the lemons.

P.E.

Outfield has the sweet green smell
of clover until you get close enough
to look for shamrocks and find
you've lost the scent and soon
you hear them shouting
screaming and calling you names
because that scary lump of leather
has landed there, a little meteor
nestled like a mushroom in the grass
right next to you. It could
have landed on your head
but the other players shriek at you
and call you rude names in Spanish
until finally the bell rings
and you know you'll be forgiven
because you alone know
the helping verbs and nine times six:
they'll need you, until P.E. tomorrow.

A Summer Place

Where I come from August is a bludgeon,
so you stay inside where the carpet looks
like chocolate ice cream and you imagine
an interesting life if the house were upside-
down and you walked on the ceiling.

Where I come from salt crusts fallow ground
and the sand under the tractor is so white
cousins in Iowa watch the yellow jumping film
and say they didn't know there was snow
in California.

Where I come from you can pick brittle shells
from coarse sand. Before people, water was here;
you can still see the mark at the mountain's knee.

Where I come from, men use chemistry to coax
citrus and grapes from porous soil, and date trees
make crisscross forests as you speed by
in a pickup with all the windows down.

Where I come from, heaven is the icy lunch bar
at the back of the Rexall, where the lady
with the beehive mixes chocolate malts, the air
smells like makeup and grilled sandwiches
and a hundred sawing strings sing
"There's a Summer Place."

The Sound of Music

At two o'clock on an August afternoon
it's 115 degrees outside, but in the theater
it's as cool as the alpine air where Maria
enthuses in the lush grass among
the edelweiss, reminding us that the hills
are alive as she and the rest of the cast
transport us for the next two hours
to a place where grass grows by itself,
there are four seasons, children
are usually blond, and real things happen.

At the end, when good has triumphed over evil
we stumble down from the mountains
of Austria and onto a concrete parking lot
in Palm Springs. Here the heat presses hard
from every angle; we know better
than to touch a car's sizzling door frame
or to sit bare-thighed on its vinyl seat.

Our mothers drive us home through
the shimmering air that rises from the asphalt;
I am both cheered and depressed to know
that there's another life somewhere
where things are clean and bright and so
much better than here in this boring land
of heat, sand, supermarket, swimming pool.

8th Grade Field Trip

The sun never came out that day on Mount San Jacinto.
We drove up in buses to hike around in fog, our teachers
taking a break from teaching so we could run free.
Greg was a magnet for us. We didn't know why,
but where he was, we needed to be. Tall, seeming older
than the rest – Adam's apple, shadowed upper lip –
he must have known some things that we needed to learn.
We followed him down trails, behind boulders, everywhere
losing him to the scarves of fog that curled around tree trunks
and filled hollows. What was this ache I felt, this pleasant
lump in my throat, this poignant longing? It wasn't the boy
exactly, or the fog, but somehow the fog and the boy together,
the fog and the boy and the mountain, the fog, the boy,
the mountain and the trees all dark and wet and shadowy
like the future drawing me in to its mysteries, the past
behind me a sunny path I would never walk again.

The Poem

At ten o'clock I get up
and into my swimsuit.
In the kitchen
my mother is talking
on the telephone.
I recognize the words –
a poem I wrote the night before
left by mistake on the table.
Now my own perfect words
mock me in singsong.
Rage rises
to my 13-year-old throat.
Barefoot, uncombed,
I throw myself outside.
The August heat engulfs me;
I stumble over the sizzling street.
My feet begin to cry
but I am deaf to them.
I don't feel the sweat
that slides along my body,
nor the bruising heat;
I jump from puddle of shade
to bristly lawn,
aware only of the bitter sawing
in my chest.
Before I reach the Denny's
on the highway,
where my body knows
there is ice water
and air sweet as January,
she drives up next to me,
opens the door. I fall
into the shade,
the cool upholstery,

to find her laughing;
it's the first time
she's ever seen me angry.

Devil Winds

Before shopping malls
    before golf courses
        before paved roads
            covered the sloping dunes,

winds like these lifted sand
                    into the air
and it took days
        to settle,
left the desert sky
      to make
a week-long shift from grey
         to taupe, then tan, then beige,
           before drifting back
to blue.

When those winds tossed your hair
it was not a caress, but a reminder:

      they could bring sandsting to the eye,
         pit a windshield,
            rip a roof from a building.

Now where I live along the coast,
    winds like these
        fly in from the desert
bringing flames
      smoke
        flying ash.

When these winds blow in,
it is not a caress;
it's an omen.

Balboa

When we were little, my buddy and I
beat a daily path down the boardwalk
to the Fun Zone and back until our soles
were black. When we were older
and cleaner, we rode the ferry and mostly
wore shoes. That summer before I began
to feel wrong, we slinked around the island
day after day. His sister told me
my pants were *outrageous* and she was cool
so I loved wearing those pants. At night,
we'd go back to the fun zone where lights
were strung and teenagers danced
to the Kinks and the Stones or stood
around the edges like us, looking in.
A boy with brown hair and pimples
on his cheeks always stared at me
and I stared back. On what must
have been his last night there he came
up close and kissed me fast on the cheek
as he walked past. We left a few days later,
back to where it was so hot and dead;
when school began I didn't feel right
in my skin. That whole year it went on,
that feeling like slipping gears, like a roller
off track. The pimple-cheeked boy
and his kiss melted slowly in my memory,
hard candy for my mind to savor.

The Weaker Sex

We laid our towels out each day before the fog broke, hugged knees to chests and waited for sun. By afternoon the beach was covered with mothers, children, and teens like us. We were the girls who looked slyly about, made clever comments to each other, waited for boys to notice us and come around. Sometimes they were college guys, or scrawny high school boys. But most often they were shorn and scrubbed sailors and marines from inland states, with sunburned backs and necks, waiting to be sent to 'Nam. When they came to us, we spoke a kind of English we made up, a language broken like twigs for kindling. Our accents were thick as syrup. We were refugees from Romania sometimes, or Russia. Not communists, but at times the boys thought we were, so we made up horror stories of our imagined home. They were going off to 'Nam to avenge the deaths of brothers or friends, or to make the world safe from communism. Most often, though, they were going off like lambs and asked no questions. We were flexing the muscles of our power, before going back to the sweet privilege of a summer home.

Before the Internet: Reading Porn at 14

I swiped it from the carousel in the back of the store
that held the pulp books, the kind with crooked type
and no pictures on the covers. At 14, I couldn't buy it
but it fit easily into my jacket pocket.
My best friend and I read it in the bathroom:
it told of a guy named Zeno and his throbbing,
veined "manhood." There was an eager red-haired
teenager with a long dong. Somewhere there was a trip
to Mexico and a scene with a woman whose body
was described as a "carcass"; there was something
there about a chocolate eclair that burst.
A five-year-old girl was brought in; after a time,
she reacted in a "womanly" way to the goings-on.
We read the book in fits and starts over several days,
each time looking at one another with horror,
flinging it away with sick stomachs. Nothing
in our experience had prepared us for this
and it did nothing to ready us for the mundane sex
of real-life. But somewhere stitched through
these scenes that shocked us so was a humor
which did not escape us, and it was the title
that had caught my eye as it gazed from the wire
shelf: "Poked and Pried Open." I wonder now
about the author, imagine a homely man
with a big imagination and a need to fund his own
writing ambitions. As for me, I became a teacher.

Awaiting Rain

When I was young
I never knew
when my period
would come.
I waited
for those rust-colored
first drops the way
the desert
awaited rain.
There were many
false alarms –
a clear, tacky sloughing
but no more –
like clouds that clotted
above the mountains
but never made it
into the valley
of dry sand
with its chafing grains,
and dry me trying
to become and remain
a woman.

The Young Ascetic

When I was seventeen we moved back
to the farm near the fault line. From my bedroom
I saw the tops of the hills that lay like stacks
of overturned books; all night I heard bullfrogs
bleating in the moonlit reservoir.

I had mastered the art of self-discipline.
I exercised every day by walking and running
among the rows of citrus. I did all my homework
on time and studied for tests. I ate only
what was absolutely necessary and only when
my stomach had stopped its grumbling; I imagined
each bite echoing as it dropped into my belly's
ravenous pit. Once every month I had dessert:
one cookie or one scoop of ice cream, which
I would eat slowly, savoring each touch of my tongue.

After a while people started to say I was too thin.
I looked at the photos and could see they were right,
but looking down at myself I knew there was still
fat to burn. I looked at women who were slim
but not skinny and wonder how they did it. Sometimes
craving sweet, I shoveled golden raisins into my mouth
and suffered the gassy consequences.

At night I lay in my bed and watched the moon rise
through my open window. In spring the flowering trees
in the orchard lit my room with their scent.
In the morning the sun peered over the pink hills
to wake me. I knew what mistakes to avoid in the life
that was ahead; meanwhile I would live my days
doing everything I felt was right as I waited,
peaceful and whole, for my real life to begin.

Vehicle

Here is my body's younger self
crouched on a rock. Those feet
are the feet by which I have trod
the earth, but the photo
was taken before living
had given them
bunions and fungus.
The hair that falls
in a hazy fan
down the shoulder
is this hair before it took on
shades of silver and gray.
The face in the photo
is turned away, watching
the winter sun settle
beyond the mountains
while the future
crouches behind the rock,
waiting to climb the young back,
this same back with the turn
in its spine which forms
the little hump where
for six decades I have stored
my slights and sorrows.
All that I have ever thought
or dreamed or done
took place within
this scaffolding of bone.

College Freshman, Home for Spring Break

My mind is full of Latin declensions,
the Norman Invasion, the poems
of John Donne. It's April, the air
sweet with citrus blossom. At breakfast

Dad asks, Will I help him hoe weeds?
This was always an honor for a male visitor,
not a daughter! It was man's work;
I never gave it a thought. It was my father

come in from the field, wiping sweat,
my brother's boots tracking sand
in the entry way. But Dad is mild now,
no more the scary hulk of my childhood.

We walk the sandy rows together,
wielding hoes, whacking. He shows me
how the blossom grows, how the petals drop,
how the green nub at the heart swells

into a lemon, an orange, a Dancy tangerine.
All the years I grew there I never
gave it a thought; it was magic I took
for granted like the daily sunrise, the wind

that rose from nothing, the alchemy
that can turn a beast of a man
into a gentle purveyor of knowledge.

The Death of the Farm

"There's no there there." – Gertrude Stein

I wasn't there those decades ago
when my father stood
on that sandy spot
near the fault line
and imagined the Valhalla
of evergreens he would plant
which every Christmas
would rustle before him
resplendent with edible ornament.

I wasn't there fifty years later
when the corporation ripped
them out of the ground
roots naked in the bright light
of spring. I wasn't there
when they hauled them off,
stacked them like corpses
and burned them. I wasn't there
to hear the roar of bulldozers,
the roots yanked from the soil –
Eureka lemons, Royal mandarins,
Orlando tangelos.

If I go there now
I will not see the paradise
my father envisioned beyond
creosote and tumbleweed,
nor the rows of trees
where jack rabbits leapt
and our dogs leapt after them;
I will only see the end
of a dead man's crazy dream,
a mirage of memory
in the bare, clawed land,
in the haunted sand.

Home

No more house
where I grew
from small,
no more the orchard
where I ran.
No more
the man and woman
who built this place,
loved and fought here,
made it home.
That home
a dusty dwelling
in my mind
a drop of land
a little refuge
built in sand.

ACKNOWLEDGEMENTS

"8th Grade Field Trip," "Awaiting Rain," and "Her Name Was Becky" appeared in *Writing in a Woman's voice.*

"Sears Catalog" was published in *Your Daily Poem.*

"The Young Ascetic" appeared in the *ME, AT 17* series from Silver Birch Press.

"The Death of the Farm" and "Bougainvillea" were previously published in the chapbook *The Belly Remembers.*

"The Salton Sea" appeared in *Galleywinter* #37.

"*En Memoria,*" "The Pink House," "The Weaker Sex," "Child Writer," and "Vehicle" were published in *Cholla Needles.*

"College Freshman, Home for Spring Break" appeared in *San Pedro River Review.*

Thank you to Donna Hilbert and Eric Morago for their help, and to all the wonderful poets in Donna Hilbert's poetry workshop whose keen eyes have informed each of these poems.

ACKNOWLEDGMENTS